THE BEATITUDES

A Guide to Good Living: Matthew 5:1-12

Phillip D. Jensen and
Tony Payne

FAITHWALK
BIBLE STUDIES

CROSSWAY BOOKS • WHEATON, ILLINOIS
A DIVISION OF GOOD NEWS PUBLISHERS

15	14	13	12	11	10	09	08	07	06	05	04	03	02	01	00	99
15	14	13	12	11	10	9	8	7	6	5	4	3	2	1		

Contents

How to Make the Most of These Studies

1. What Is an Interactive Bible Study?

These "interactive" Bible studies are a bit like a guided tour of a famous city. The studies will take you through each of the Beatitudes, pointing out things along the way, filling in background details, and suggesting avenues for further exploration. But there is also time for you to do some sightseeing of your own—to wander off, have a good look for yourself, and form your own conclusions.

In other words, we have designed these studies to fall halfway between a sermon and a set of unadorned Bible study questions. We want to provide input and point you in the right direction, while leaving you to do a lot of the exploration and discovery yourself.

We hope that these studies will stimulate lots of interaction—interaction with the Bible, with the things we've written, with your own current thoughts and attitudes, with other people as you study with them, and with God as you talk to Him about it all.

2. The Format

Each study focuses on a Beatitude and contains sections of text to introduce, summarize, suggest, and provoke. Interspersed throughout the text are three types of "interaction," each with its own symbol:

STARTING OUT

Questions to help you think about society and your own experience, in a way that tunes you in to the issues being raised by the Bible passage.

 FINDING TRUTH

Questions to help you investigate key parts of the Bible.

GOING FURTHER

Questions to help you think through the implications of your discoveries.

When you come to one of these symbols, you'll know that it's time to do some work on your own.

3. Suggestions for Individual Study

▲ Before you begin, pray that God would open your eyes to what He is saying in the Beatitudes and give you the spiritual strength to do something about it. You may be spurred to pray again at the end of the study.

▲ Work through the study, following the directions as you go. Write in the spaces provided.

▲ Resist the temptation to skip over the *Starting Out, Finding Truth,* and *Going Further* sections. It is important to think about the sections of text (rather than just accepting them as true) and to ponder the implications for your life. Writing these things down is a valuable way to get your thoughts working.

▲ Take what opportunities you can to talk with others about what you've learned.

4. Suggestions for Group Study

▲ Much of what we have suggested above applies to group study as well. The studies are suitable for structured Bible study or cell groups, as well as for more informal pairs and threesomes.

Get together with one or more friends and work on the studies at your own pace. You don't need the formal structure of a "group" to gain maximum benefit.

▲ It is vital that group members work through the study themselves *before* the group meets. The group discussion can take place comfortably in an hour (depending on how sidetracked you get!), but only if all the members have done the work and are familiar with the material.

▲ Spend most of the group time discussing the "interactive" sections—*Starting Out, Finding Truth,* and *Going Further.* Reading all the text together would take too long and should be unnecessary if the group members have done their preparation. You may wish to underline and read aloud particular paragraphs or sections of text that you think are important.

▲ The role of the group leader is to direct the course of the discussion and try to draw the threads together at the end. This will mean a little extra preparation—underlining important sections of text to emphasize, deciding which questions are worth concentrating on, being sure of the main thrust of the study. Leaders will also probably want to decide approximately how long they'd like to spend on each part.

▲ We haven't included an "answer guide" to the questions in the studies. This is a deliberate move. We want to give you a guided tour of the Beatitudes, not a lecture. There is more than enough in the text we have written and the questions we have asked to point you in what we think is the right direction. The rest is up to you.

1

A Guide to Good Living

Before we launch into studying the individual Beatitudes, we need to step back and look at the bigger picture. What are the Beatitudes all about? How should we approach them?

(Incidentally, the word *Beatitude* is not in the Bible—it is just a title that some people have given to these verses. It comes from the Latin word *beatus*, meaning "blessed." It has no direct correlation with our English word *attitude*.)

1. The Rest of the Picture

A man sees an odd-shaped piece of animal skin on the ground in front of him. He lashes out at it with his foot and sends it skimming across the open, grassy field on which he is standing. As a direct consequence of his action, several million people around the world experience intense feelings of joy or despair.

This sounds crazy . . . until we fill in the rest of the picture. The rest of the picture is that the open grassy field is a soccer stadium, the man is the finest soccer player of his time, and the scene is the final game of the World Cup soccer tournament.

Words and actions taken out of context are often meaningless. And this is one of the main mistakes we make in reading the Bible— we take the words (and the actions they describe) out of their original context. Far too frequently, we read our own concerns back into the Bible, rather than letting it speak for itself in its own setting.

To fill in the rest of the picture surrounding the Beatitudes, we need to look at three different areas.

The Biblical Context

In the context of the whole Bible, the Sermon on the Mount occurred at a time when the fortunes of Israel were at a low ebb.

There had been a time when this was not so—under David and Solomon, Israel had been a safe and prosperous nation. According to His promises to Abraham, God had planted them in the Promised Land, subdued their enemies, and blessed them with prosperity. This was the historical high point of Israel as a nation.

From that point on, however, things went downhill, until eventually Israel was destroyed because of its chronic apostasy and rebellion against God. By the time of the Exile to Babylon in 587 B.C., the everlasting kingdom promised to David in 2 Samuel 7 was in ruins (see Ps. 89).

But all was not lost. God's promise to Abraham still stood. As Israel's fortunes declined, the prophets emphatically declared that God would restore His kingdom.

 FINDING TRUTH

Read Isaiah 9:1-7.

1. What did the prophet look forward to?

2. What sort of kingdom would the "child" rule over?

3. Now read Matthew 4:12-17. How did Jesus fulfill Isaiah's prophecy?

The Old Testament looked forward to a day when the eternal kingdom of God would be established throughout the world, and it would be presided over by "one like a Son of Man" (Dan. 7:13; see also Isa. 11:1-10; Ezek. 34:23ff.).

The message of the New Testament is that Jesus gloriously fulfilled this hope. Jesus says as much in our Sermon: "Do not think that I have come to abolish the Law or the Prophets; I have not come to abolish them but to fulfill them" (Matt. 5:17).

The Beatitudes, then, come at a pivotal point in God's plan of salvation. The Messiah has come; the kingdom of God is at hand. However, not all has yet been accomplished. The Cross, the Resurrection, the outpouring of the Spirit at Pentecost—these momentous events are still to come, and we live on the other side of them.

The Historical Context

What was life like at the time of Jesus? What would have been in the minds of His hearers as they listened to His teaching?

No doubt there were many things in their minds, and we can only guess at what those might have been. However, of one thing we can be fairly sure. The Jews of Jesus' day were sick of being losers. Nearly five centuries had passed since the last of the Old Testament prophets, and during that period, with a few exceptions, Israel had suffered nothing but humiliation at the hands of the Gentiles (first the Greeks and then the Romans). In Jesus' day, the brutal fact of Roman occupation could not be avoided, and different groups within Israel had ideas about how God was going to bring in His kingdom.

The Pharisees, on the whole, felt that God would not bring in His kingdom until Israel got serious about obeying the Law. They were quite fanatical about keeping God's commandments in the Old Testament Scriptures, as well as the countless man-made regulations that had accrued over the centuries. However, from what we learn of the Pharisees in the Gospels, the obedience they taught was external, legalistic, and hypocritical. It did not touch the heart.

Other groups, whom we might call the "nationalists," thought that military action was the way to usher in God's kingdom. They were in favor of overthrowing the Romans by force and setting up a new nation under God. (In fact, they tried this on a couple of occasions during the first century A.D., and lost.)

The Jews were a downtrodden people. They inwardly seethed at the humiliation of being governed by Gentiles, and they sorrowed at the sad state into which God's chosen people had fallen.

However, it must also be said that there were some in Israel who were not so worried about the Romans being in control. The Sadducees, for instance, were the ruling upper class of Israelite society. They had a cozy political relationship with the Romans and had no real interest in having the situation disturbed. There were other Jews who had made a lot of money under Roman rule, and they also were quite happy for things to stay the way they were.

Into this mixed environment of messianic hope strode Jesus, proclaiming that the time had finally come—the kingdom of God was at hand.

The Context in Matthew

This is something you can look up for yourself.

 FINDING TRUTH

Read Matthew 4:17–5:2; 7:28-29.

1. What did Jesus preach?

2. What did He call His disciples to do?

3. To whom did Jesus preach the Sermon?

2. The Message of the Sermon

Now that we have looked at the wider picture, the overall message of the Sermon comes into focus. Jesus has begun His public ministry and has called His disciples. He sits down with them and begins to teach them how they are to live as subjects in the long-awaited kingdom of God. He is giving them their first "discipleship training" session.

He tells them that they are a select band, called to be the light of the world, just as He Himself has come as a light (see 4:15-16). He tells them that if they are to enter His kingdom, their righteousness must far exceed the external, legalistic acts of the Pharisees. They must have a deep-seated, internal commitment to God that is expressed by doing His will. They must listen to Jesus' words and obey them, even though it may make them completely different from the rest of their society.

This theme of "being different" crops up again and again in the Sermon. Whether talking about the Pharisees or the pagans, Jesus stresses that the kingdom-dweller must give his or her allegiance to the king. He must abandon the foolish and self-centered attitudes of those around him. It is for this reason that John Stott regards 6:8—"Do not be like them"—as the key text of the Sermon (see his commentary on the Sermon on the Mount in *The Bible Speaks Today* series). Jesus is calling His disciples to a radical set of values that will bring them into conflict with their friends and family and society.

Even though the Sermon is directed primarily at the disciples, the crowds are also listening in. In many ways, the message is the same

for them. If they are to enter Jesus' kingdom, they must seek it whole-
heartedly and be prepared for a complete life-change.

3. A Guide to Good Living

If this is the general message of the whole Sermon on the Mount,
what is the place of the first twelve verses, which we call the
Beatitudes?

The Beatitudes outline the good life, the blessed life, the life of
one who participates in the kingdom that Jesus brings. They are, in
many respects, a "guide to good living." They describe the person
whom God esteems, the one who is to be envied. This is what the
word *blessed* means. To be blessed is to receive good things from God.

The eight blessings of the Beatitudes do not describe eight different people—as if there are some of us who are merciful, others who
are poor in spirit, and others who are peacemakers. They are not eight
different classes of people, but the one person—the blessed person—
who has found real life.

The Beatitudes present us with two exciting challenges:

The *first* challenge is to understand these very familiar words
afresh, to find out what Jesus was really saying all those centuries ago.
To do this, we will have to do something that many of us find difficult, but which is absolutely necessary if we are going to understand what Jesus was saying. We will have to dig back into the Old
Testament.

It is easy to go astray at this point. The Beatitudes themselves
are very short and pithy. They do not provide much explanation. It
is tempting to make up for this by picking our way through the New
Testament to find what else it teaches (e.g., about mourning or meekness), and then read this back into Matthew 5 to explain what Jesus
must have meant.

While this is a worthwhile exercise, it really is coming at the
Beatitudes from the wrong direction. The key to unlocking the treas-
ures of these well-known verses is found by looking backwards, to
what came before, to the Old Testament. For these are not a new set
of values. Each of the eight "blessings" echoes the teaching of the Old
Testament. Jesus was quite clear on this point: "Do not think that I
have come to abolish the Law and the Prophets; I have not come to
abolish them but to fulfill them" (5:17).

As you work through this book, you'll find that we have used this pattern of Old Testament hope and New Testament fulfillment as the basis of the studies. Each study has the following structure, with minor variations:

1. The hope (from the Old Testament)

2. The fulfillment (in Jesus)

3. Good living (how this should affect our lives in Jesus' kingdom)

The Old Testament looked forward to a time when God would again bless His people. In Jesus, and in these "Beatitudes," we see the fulfillment of that hope.

The *second* challenge is to repent. The Beatitudes have hard things to say to us, things that cut through the comfort and complacency that often mark our Christian lives. As we have already seen, the Sermon on the Mount calls on us to be *different* from those around us. It challenges us to live God's way, even though that might turn our values and ideas upside down.

Let us approach these well-known words of Jesus with the attitude expressed in the final chapter of Isaiah:

> *"This is the one I esteem:*
> *he who is humble and contrite in spirit,*
> *and trembles at my word."*
> —Isaiah 66:2

 GOING FURTHER

1. How did Jesus fulfill the expectations of the Old Testament about the One who was to come?

2. How did He challenge or frustrate the expectations of the Jews of His time?

Read through the Beatitudes.
3. On first reading, how do you think they might challenge the expectations we have of what it means to be a Christian?

The Privilege of the Poor

"Blessed are the poor in spirit,
for theirs is the kingdom of heaven."
—Matthew 5:3

What "blessing" is there in being poor?

There is certainly no blessing in being financially poor. Anyone who has known genuine poverty will know that it is a crushing, humiliating experience. If money is power, then the poor are powerless, and their powerlessness is often exploited. Without the means to improve their situation, the poor pass this predicament on to their children. Being poor is no fun.

Jesus seems to think that poverty is a desirable state, but what sort of poverty is He referring to? It is not simply economic poverty— the addition of "in spirit" makes that clear. But what does it mean to be "poor in spirit"? Does it imply a shortage of the Holy Spirit? Or a general lack of human spirit—like a kind of spiritual wimp? Or is it something else? As we have already suggested, the key to understanding Jesus' meaning lies in the Old Testament.

The theme of riches and poverty keeps popping up throughout the Old Testament in numerous contexts. Among this diversity of material, our particular interest is in how riches and poverty relate to the "kingdom," for this is what Jesus is promising in this Beatitude —that the poor in spirit will possess the kingdom of heaven.

In the Old Testament, being "poor" meant a lot more than simply being short of cash. The word *poor* became a much broader description of lowliness and godliness, and this is hardly surprising. Those who don't have much money tend to trust in God, for they have no one else to turn to. They are only too aware of their need and of their true status before God. There is no pride or self-sufficiency to stand in their way, and God esteems them for this.

The opposite is also true. Rich people tend to be arrogant and proud. They are used to being treated with respect, to getting their own way, to being "someone." They have no need of God, or so they think. As we shall see, this was especially true in the Exile in Babylon.

1. The Hope—Riches in God's Kingdom

The first thing we must recognize is that God is the owner and source of all riches. He is the sovereign Lord, who blesses people with riches as He sees fit:

> *"The LORD sends poverty and wealth;*
> *he humbles and he exalts.*
> *He raises the poor from the dust*
> *and lifts the needy from the ash heap;*
> *he seats them with princes*
> *and has them inherit a throne of honor."*
> —1 Samuel 2:7-8

> *The blessing of the LORD brings wealth,*
> *and he adds no trouble to it.*
> —Proverbs 10:22

One of God's promises to Israel was that He would make her a prosperous and wealthy nation. Even in the process of rescuing Israel from Egypt, God blessed them with plunder from the Egyptians (Ex. 12:35-36), and then brought them to the Promised Land, a land of great wealth "flowing with milk and honey" (Deut. 8:7-10). By the time of King David and King Solomon, Israel was a great and prosperous kingdom.

The wealth and prosperity of Israel in this period is illustrated in the preparations for the building of the temple. Vast quantities of gold, silver, bronze, and iron were willingly given by David and the leaders and officials of Israel, prompting David to rejoice and thank God for the riches He had given them:

> *"Now, our God, we give you thanks,*
> *and praise your glorious name.*

"But who am I, and who are my people, that we should be able to give as generously as this? Everything comes from you, and we have given you only what comes from your hand. We are aliens and strangers in your sight, as were all our forefathers. Our days on earth are like a shadow, without hope. O LORD our God, as for all this abundance that we have provided for building you a temple for your Holy Name, it comes from your hand, and all of it belongs to you."

—1 Chronicles 29:13-16

The glory of David and Solomon was a high point for the kingdom of God in the Old Testament. From that time on, however, everything went downhill. Instead of thanking God for the blessings of wealth and serving Him faithfully, Israel turned aside to other gods. Although they were warned not to, they forgot the Lord who had brought them out of Egypt and blessed them with prosperity (see Deut. 8:1-20).

God's judgment fell on Israel. The northern part of the kingdom was wiped out by the Assyrians in 722 B.C. and the remaining two tribes (Judah and Benjamin) were routed and dragged off into Exile by Babylon in 587. The riches that God had given them were now in the hands of foreigners. They were dispossessed, exiled, poor.

 FINDING TRUTH

Two of the big themes of Isaiah are the judgment that is about to fall on Israel because of her wickedness, and the salvation and comfort that God will bring to His people after He has judged them.

Read Isaiah 9:8–10:4.

1. What had God already done to Israel?

2. What was Israel's attitude in response?

3. How was Israel (as a whole) using its wealth?

4. What did Isaiah prophesy would happen to Israel?

Now read Isaiah 61:1-7.
5. What is the good news that will be preached to the poor?

6. Who is going to free the captives and proclaim the year of God's favor?

7. How do you think this prophecy might relate to the ministry of Jesus? (Compare Matt. 4:13-17, Luke 4:17-21, and this Beatitude in Matt. 5:3.)

Poor in Spirit: Being humble in Spirit.

Jesus was the greatest person who ever lived, yet the most humble.

Not all God's people in Babylon were "poor." Some managed to do very nicely for themselves, but only by *compromising*. Those who sold out to the Babylonians, who adopted their culture and their pagan ways, were able to become quite wealthy. When the time came to return to Judah to rebuild the shattered ruins of Jerusalem, they didn't want to go.

In the context of Isaiah 61, the poor were the exiled people of Israel who had not compromised but still longed for God to rescue them from their poverty and shame. They were dispossessed, without resources or hope. The kingdom of David was in ruins, and the riches God had once blessed them with were gone. The poor were those who, out of their poverty, longed for God to save them and establish (or reestablish) His glorious kingdom. The Old Testament looked forward to this time, when the poor would be lifted up from their lowly position and would "feed on the wealth of nations" (Isa. 61:6).

2. The Fulfillment—The Way of Poverty

By the time of Jesus and the New Testament, several hundred years had elapsed. Israel had continued to suffer at the hands of foreign overlords, though perhaps not quite to the extent that they had during the Exile. There were still those among the people who longed for the promised kingdom to come, when Isaiah's prophecy would be fulfilled and the riches of God's kingdom would be theirs.

These people were the "poor in spirit" upon whom Jesus pronounces a blessing in Matthew 5. They had no attachment to the riches and possessions of this world. They longed for God to intervene in history and set up His worldwide kingdom.

But there were also those in New Testament Israel who had done very well and were rich. Just as in the Exile, they were the compromisers. Was it possible to be a wealthy Jew during the Roman occupation of Palestine and still be faithful to God? Possible, but extremely unlikely. In the New Testament, the classic rich people are the Sadducees and the tax collectors, and both groups gained their wealth by selling out to the pagan oppressors. They had too much to gain from the current situation to want it to change. They didn't want God to establish His kingdom and remove the source of their income! What was it that Jesus said about camels and the eyes of needles?

This contrast between the godly poor and the compromised rich is recorded a number of times in the ministry of Jesus.

FINDING TRUTH

Read Luke 18:9–19:9.

1. As you read this succession of incidents, note down the characteristics of those who:

    ▲ were accepted by God or saved or blessed

    ▲ did not receive salvation/blessing

It is significant that Jesus established the kingdom of God by becoming poor Himself. There is no reason to think that Jesus' family was particularly poor, since carpentry was a fairly normal middle-class profession in the first century. However, Christ's life as an itinerant preacher was one in which food, sleep, and shelter were probably lacking (see Mark 4:36-38; 11:12):

> *"Foxes have holes and birds of the air have nests, but the Son of Man has no place to lay his head."*
>
> —Luke 9:58

More than this, Jesus *became poor* by entering our world:

> *For you know the grace of our Lord Jesus Christ, that though he was rich, yet for your sakes he became poor, so that you through his poverty might become rich.*
>
> —2 Corinthians 8:9; see also Philippians 2:5-11

More still, Jesus became poor by dying on the Cross. He vacated the splendor of heaven for the poverty of our condemnation. He emptied Himself and became as nothing, in order to make us rich. It is not surprising, then, that Jesus' teaching is full of this idea. The path of poverty was not only Jesus' path into the world and to the Cross, it was also to be the way for His disciples.

This, then, is the character of the Christian. Those who are lowly and poor in spirit will possess the kingdom of heaven. God does not favor the rich and powerful, but those who call on Him out of their great need. This is the very nature of the Gospel. It is a weak and foolish Gospel—the word of the Cross—which shames the wise and the strong (see 1 Cor. 1:18-31).

Those who trust in this Gospel receive the riches of the kingdom of heaven, in fulfillment of the Old Testament hope. Paul prays for the Ephesians that they might know or realize just how rich they are in Christ; he wants their eyes to be opened to the inheritance God has in store for them in heaven (Eph. 1:18). We see this perspective at a number of places in the New Testament. In Christ we have true riches, regardless of our financial status. The riches of the Gospel should change the way we think of ourselves:

> *The brother in humble circumstances ought to take pride in his high position. But the one who is rich should take pride in his low position, because he will pass away like a wild flower.*
> —James 1:9-10

> *"I know your afflictions and your poverty—yet you are rich!"*
> —Revelation 2:9

> *"You say, 'I am rich; I have acquired wealth and do not need a thing.' But you do not realize that you are wretched, pitiful, poor, blind and naked. I counsel you to buy from me gold refined in the fire, so you can become rich; and white clothes to wear, so you can cover your shameful nakedness; and salve to put on your eyes, so you can see."*
> —Revevelation 3:17-18

3. Good Living—Rich and Poor

If the Old Testament hope was for riches, and we have received those riches spiritually in Christ, how then should we live? The answer is: as rich . . . and yet poor.

In Christ, we are rich indeed. All the riches and wealth of the kingdom are ours, kept in heaven for us, and already tasted by us in our relationship with God. This should lift us up and cause us to rejoice and praise God.

In another sense, however, we are still to live as "poor" people. The good life, says Jesus, is to be "poor in spirit," dependent on God, not compromising ourselves with worldly riches. It is very hard to long for God's kingdom and to put our trust in Him when we are rich. Riches breed arrogance and pride and a spirit of self-sufficiency. This is the point of the comparisons that are made in Luke 18 (the passage we investigated earlier).

At this point, we have to be honest with ourselves. We Western Christians find wealth particularly deceptive. Very few people in our society would regard themselves as rich, but most of us are. We might prefer the label "middle-class," but in relative terms we are among the wealthiest people the world has ever seen.

Our wealth or poverty affects how we think of ourselves and how we approach God. Most Western Christians have been brought up to believe that power, knowledge, wealth, and achievement are the things worth having. They would perhaps rewrite this Beatitude to read, "Blessed are the rich and powerful, for theirs is the kingdom on earth."

This is a spiritual hurdle for us. It is hard to be poor in spirit when we are rich in goods and possessions. This is Jesus' point later in the Sermon, when He says:

> "Do not store up for yourselves treasures on earth, where moth and rust destroy, and where thieves break in and steal. But store up for yourselves treasures in heaven, where moth and rust do not destroy, and where thieves do not break in and steal. For where your treasure is, there your heart will be also. . . . No one can serve two masters. Either he will hate the one and love the other, or he will be devoted to the one and despise the other. You cannot serve both God and Money."
>
> —Matthew 6:19-21, 24

We need to examine ourselves on this issue. Are our possessions distorting our relationship with God? Are we compromising? How are we using the wealth that God has given us?

To be poor in spirit when all around is arrogance, compromise, and self-indulgence—this is the radically good lifestyle Jesus calls us to.

 **GOING FURTHER**

1. Summarize the main things you have learned about:

   ▲ poverty

   ▲ Jesus

2. How might being "poor in spirit" affect

   ▲ the way you pray?

   ▲ the way you relate to other people?

3. Do you think of yourself primarily as a rich or poor person, or as neither?

4. Are your possessions affecting your relationship with God?

5. Do you have a problem with pride or arrogance? How does it show itself?

The Pleasure of the Mourners

> "Blessed are those who mourn,
> for they will be comforted."
> —Matthew 5:4

The promise of this second Beatitude—that those who mourn will be comforted—is one of the strangest in the Bible. What does it mean to mourn? And how will the mourner be comforted? Does it mean that God will particularly bless the bereaved?

In Luke 2, we read of some mourners, but not of the kind that hang around funeral parlors. When Joseph and Mary take their baby son Jesus up to Jerusalem to be circumcised, they encounter two elderly people at the temple:

> Now there was a man in Jerusalem called Simeon, who was righteous and devout. He was waiting for the consolation of Israel, and the Holy Spirit was upon him. . . .
>
> There was also a prophetess, Anna, the daughter of Phanuel. . . . She never left the temple but worshipped night and day, fasting and praying. Coming up to them [Joseph and Mary], . . . she gave thanks to God and spoke about the child to all who were looking forward to the redemption of Jerusalem.
>
> —Luke 2:25, 36-38

In due course we will see that Simeon and Anna are classic examples of what Jesus means by "those who mourn." As in our last study, the place to start is with Jesus' Bible—the Old Testament.

1. The Hope—"O Jerusalem!"

In the Old Testament, a single event is unquestionably the focus of Israel's mourning. That event is the Exile to Babylon.

In 587 B.C. the Babylonian king Nebuchadnezzar laid siege to Jerusalem, finally destroying the city and its temple and carrying off the inhabitants to Babylon. It was a national catastrophe.

The book of Lamentations is a response to this tragedy.

 FINDING TRUTH

Read Lamentations 1:1–2:5.

1. Write down some of the words and phrases the author uses to describe the emotional reactions to what has happened.

2. What is the reason given for Israel's disgrace?

3. Now read the following prophetic passages. In each case, what do the prophets look forward to?

    ▲ Isaiah 40:1-5

    ▲ Isaiah 61:1-7

    ▲ Jeremiah 31:1-14

Israel *was* restored from Babylon, at least partially. The bulk of the people did return and the temple was rebuilt, even if not to its former glory.

However, the glowing expectations of the prophets were not met. Israel continued to suffer under foreign overlords—first Persia, then Greece, and then (in New Testament times) Rome.

In Jesus' time, there were still those, like Simeon and Anna, who mourned for the sorry state of Israel and longed for God's comfort and redemption.

2. The Fulfillment—Comfort at Last

At first glance, we twentieth-century people interpret "comfort for mourners" to mean "warm, reassuring feelings for sad people." But given the Old Testament background that we have just looked at, we can see that Jesus is promising something far more significant. He is saying that God is about to fulfill the promise that Israel has been waiting for—the promise of comfort amid all their sorrows and troubles.

Because of her sin, Israel had been rejected by God. She had suffered under foreign rule for hundreds of years. The temple had been defiled, and Gentiles sat on the throne of David. Those in Israel who were concerned for God's name mourned at how His chosen people had been brought so low. Jesus Himself was a mourner for Jerusalem:

> *"O Jerusalem, Jerusalem, you who kill the prophets and stone those sent to you, how often I have longed to gather your children together, as a hen gathers her chicks under her wings, but you were not willing!"*
>
> —Luke 13:34

> *As he approached Jerusalem and saw the city, he wept over it and said, "If you, even you, had only known on this day what would bring you peace—but now it is hidden from your eyes."*
>
> —Luke 19:41-42

Jesus wept over Jerusalem, over her stubbornness and rebellion. Yet He also came to bring comfort to all those who mourned for Jerusalem. He came promising the arrival of a new age in which things would be put right, an age when the godless would be overthrown and God's kingdom would be established forever. His people would no longer suffer humiliation and indignity. They would now enjoy God's favor, as Jeremiah promised:

> *"I will turn their mourning into gladness;*
> *I will give them comfort and joy instead of sorrow."*
> —Jeremiah 31:13

This is the "consolation" Simeon looked forward to, and which had arrived in the person of Jesus.

Who will receive this consolation? Only the mourners. It is important to realize that, from the Exile right through to Jesus' time, not all Jews mourned the sad state into which Israel had fallen. Many were quite satisfied with the status quo and found interaction with the foreign occupying forces stimulating and profitable.

During the Exile, some found the good life in Babylon too hard to resist. They enjoyed the prosperity and culture of Babylonian society and had no interest in returning to Judah to rebuild their shattered nation from scratch. When the opportunity came to return, many passed it by. They weren't mourners, and consequently they didn't receive God's blessing.

Under the Greeks (during the late fourth and third centuries B.C.), many Jews embraced the sophistication and civilization of Greek culture. They enjoyed the language and theater, and especially the sporting and social centers called *gymnasia*.

Under Rome, some sections of Jewish society obtained great wealth and power and were obliged to keep Rome happy in order to maintain their position. They actively discouraged any talk of God "restoring His kingdom" for fear of antagonizing their Roman overlords.

Simeon and Anna, then, were not necessarily the norm. They were among those who were dissatisfied with their current situation and longed for God to fulfill His promise. They were looking for a change.

Jesus came announcing that the time for the change had come. He was able to promise comfort for the mourners, just as Isaiah and the other prophets had foretold.

3. Good Living—Mourning and Comfort

Jesus says that the mourners are blessed, because they will receive comfort. Their yearning for a better world, and their dissatisfaction with this world, will be satisfied. In His own day, this was tied to the sorry state of Israel. But how does it apply to us?

We have the enormous privilege of experiencing the comfort that Jesus promised. Through His death and resurrection, Jesus has ushered in the kingdom that the mourners were waiting for. We can now experience the supreme comfort of having our sins forgiven and being guaranteed a place in the world in which there will be no tears. This is part of the "good life" that the kingdom of God offers to those who enter it.

However, there is also a "not yet" element to this promise. We have entered the kingdom that Jesus brought, but we still long for its consummation. We still live in what the New Testament calls "this present evil age" with all its ungodliness, injustice, and suffering. There are still good reasons to mourn.

We should mourn over the tragic state of our world, over those among our family and friends who are lost, and over our own sin. Like Anna and Simeon, we should yearn for the day when all will be put right and God will appear in all His glory.

 GOING FURTHER

1. Summarize what Jesus meant by "those who mourn."

2. How did God fulfill His promise to comfort the mourners?

3. Would you describe people in general as "mourners"? If not, how would you describe them?

4. What is there to mourn about in

   ▲ the world?

   ▲ our own lives?

5. How do you think our mourning (or lack of it) will affect our grasp of the "comfort" God offers?

mourn— those who are sensitive/acknowledge the tragic state of this world and the sin in their lives and those who are lost.

The Strength of the Meek

> "*Blessed are the meek,*
> *for they will inherit the earth.*"
> —Matthew 5:5

The message daubed on the wall said it all: "The meek shall inherit the earth . . . if that's all right with the rest of you."

In our society, power is prized almost above all else. Even money is just a liquid form of power. People seek power in the workplace, in politics, in business, and in personal relationships. Those of us who have given up hope of ever being very powerful content ourselves with following or supporting powerful people.

Christians pursue power too, not only in the worldly sense of wanting large, powerful churches, but also "spiritually" in the current fascination with miraculous signs and wonders.

In this climate, meekness as a character trait is hardly the flavor of the month.

So who are these "meek" people that Jesus says will be blessed? How will they inherit the earth? And what does it mean for us? These are the questions we will examine in this study.

STARTING OUT

1. Before we look at what Jesus might have meant by being "meek," what do you think is the normal twentieth-century meaning of the word?

2. Is being meek a positive characteristic these days?

The word translated "meek" in Matthew 5:5 is a little hard to define precisely. It encompasses a number of ideas, such as gentleness and humility, as well as the self-control that makes these possible. Elsewhere in the New Testament, the word is used to describe an absence of aggression or pretension: "Always be prepared to give an answer . . . for the hope that you have. But do this with *gentleness* and respect" (1 Peter 3:15). Jesus uses the word in describing Himself as being "*gentle* and humble in heart" (Matt. 11:29).

1. The Hope—Inheriting the Land

What did Jesus mean by "meek" in our Beatitude in Matthew 5? The answer lies in Psalm 37, which Jesus seems to be quoting. Verse 11 of the psalm says: "But the meek will inherit the land and enjoy great peace."

Let's look more closely at this psalm.

 FINDING TRUTH

Read Psalm 37. (If you're in a group, try reading a few verses each.)

1. Look at verses 1-11. What is the right response when evil apparently triumphs over good?

2. What will God do for the meek?

3. Look at verses 12-24 and fill in the following table:

	The wicked	The righteous
Behavior		
Consequences		

Reread verses 25-40.

4. As David looks back on his long life, what is his conclusion about evil and righteous people?

5. Looking back through the whole psalm, what attitude do the meek have:

▲ toward God?

▲ toward their current situation?

2. The Fulfillment—A Better Land

In Psalm 37, the meek are promised that they will inherit "the land"—that is, the land promised to Abraham, the land of Israel in which they were now living. Even though wicked and ruthless people may have disinherited them or seized their property, the meek will in God's time possess their inheritance. The land will be theirs.

If Jesus is quoting this psalm, and it seems that He is, then what is He promising His disciples as they sit listening to Him on the mountainside? We need to remember that Jesus is talking to a Jewish audience under Roman rule. They long to be free of their overlords and to "possess the land" once more for themselves. In fact, the word usually translated "earth" in verse 5 could just as well be translated "land"—and in view of Psalm 37 it probably should be.

At one level, it seems that Jesus is saying that freedom for the Jewish people will not be achieved by violent military action or insurrection, but that, according to the Old Testament promise, God will vindicate those who wait for Him in godly dependence. He will give the land to the meek, not to the powerful.

This leaves us with some questions: How did Jesus achieve this? Did the meek ever "inherit the land" as Jesus promised? And what does it mean for us today?

The answer to these questions becomes clear if we pause to consider the relationship between the Old and New Testaments. In the Old Testament, the location of God's kingdom was a physical nation—Israel. He chose a people out of all the peoples in the ancient world, rescued them from slavery in Egypt, and took them to the land He had chosen. Israel "inherited" this land.

In the New Testament, God's people are not a physical "nation"—they are gathered from all nations and tongues. And the "land" that they inherit is not a physical plot of ground—it is heaven itself. This is the message of Hebrews 3–4. In these important chapters, the writer explains that the Old Testament land that God gave Israel is a type or forerunner of the inheritance He gives us in Christ. God has rescued us from slavery (to sin) and is leading us through this life to our great inheritance in heaven.

In this Beatitude, Jesus is promising that those who meekly wait on God will be blessed, for they will "inherit the land." Peter and John and the rest of the disciples probably didn't understand the full extent of Jesus' promise, but looking at it from our side of the Cross, we can understand it. We can see how, through His death and resurrection, Jesus has rescued His people from the ultimate slavery and oppression and has given us "an inheritance that can never perish, spoil or fade—kept in heaven for you, who through faith are shielded by God's power until the coming of the salvation that is ready to be revealed in the last time" (1 Peter 1:4-5).

3. Good Living—Meek But Not Mild

How does all this affect us as kingdom-dwellers?

First, we can praise God for the inheritance He has given us. Through the Gospel we become "heirs of God and co-heirs with Christ" (Rom. 8:17). We are citizens of heaven (Phil. 3:20) and we should pray, like Paul, that God would open our eyes to see how rich and glorious our inheritance is (Eph. 1:18).

We should also note that, just as Jesus promised, we receive this inheritance in *meekness*—that is, by trusting God. We can't force God's hand. We take our place in His kingdom only by meekly entrusting ourselves to His goodness and grace.

All this helps enormously in dealing with the frustrations and injustices of everyday life. With the knowledge of our eternal inheritance fixed in our minds, we can face the evil of our world with a degree of serenity. We can put into practice the opening words of Psalm 37:

> *Do not fret because of evil men*
> *or be envious of those who do wrong;*
> *for like the grass they will soon wither,*
> *like green plants they will soon die away.*

To be meek and trusting, when all around is wickedness, injustice, and exploitation—this is the radically good lifestyle Jesus calls us to.

 GOING FURTHER

1. Try to write a definition of what Jesus might have meant by "meek."

- blessed are the gentles (meek)

- relax & trust in GOD

2. What is our "inheritance" as Christians?

3. What things do you sometimes feel you miss out on by being a Christian?

4. How does your own character compare with Jesus' description of the meek person?

5. Try to think of some situations when you have been anything but meek.

6. Are there attitudes or behaviors you need to change?

7. The meek of Psalm 37 were exhorted to stay calm in the face of the apparent victory of the wicked. Are there ways in which this applies to you?

The Satisfaction of the Righteous

*"Blessed are those who hunger and thirst for righteousness,
for they will be filled."*

—Matthew 5:6

Hunger and thirst are powerful drives. But they are drives that we Westerners barely understand. Most of us have never known real hunger or thirst, apart from the Forty-Hour Famine we did in high school. We don't appreciate the power of hunger and thirst as images of wanting something desperately.

In fact, our society has such an abundance of food and drink that when advertisers want to sell it to us, they have to appeal to motives and drives other than simple hunger or thirst—the most common, of course, being sex and the desire for popularity.

In the public sense, there is also little hungering for righteousness in America. Compared with many other cultures, we are relatively free of oppression and tyranny. In countries where injustice is entrenched, the thirst for justice is intense. There is not that sense in America most of the time. This is true individually as well. We take for granted the spiritual benefits of living in a society that has been soaked in the Gospel of Jesus for 2,000 years.

You might note that so far I have been using the words *righteousness* and *justice* almost interchangeably. There is a good reason for this. In the Bible (and we will look at some examples shortly) righteousness is not simply a matter of personal morality—it is being rightly related to God and each other, both individually and socially.

As has been our custom, let's start to work out what Jesus was saying in this Beatitude by investigating the Old Testament background.

1. The Hope—A Righteous Kingdom

 **FINDING TRUTH**

Read Matthew 4:12-17.

1. Where does Jesus' ministry begin to take place?

2. What significance does the location have?

3. Now look up Isaiah 9:1-7, which is quoted in Matthew 4. The light that dawns in Galilee is a child that is born. What sort of kingdom/government will this child usher in?

4. Now read Isaiah 51:1-6. What will happen when God brings righteousness to Israel?

5. Based on these sorts of Old Testament promises and hopes, what sort of "righteousness" do you think the people of Jesus' day would have been looking for?

6. What do you think Jesus would have meant by "hungering and thirsting for righteousness"?

2. The Fulfillment—A Dying King

Our tendency as modern Christians is to separate Jesus' words from their setting. When we read about those who "hunger and thirst for righteousness" we immediately think that Jesus is referring to a quest for personal holiness and morality. And this is certainly part of His meaning.

However, as we have seen from our brief look at the Old Testament, Israel was looking forward to a time when all the wrongs would be put right, when injustice and oppression (particularly by Gentile powers like Greece and Rome) would come to an end, and God would establish a just and righteous kingdom with His just and righteous King on the throne.

In other words, those who were hungry for righteousness were not much different from those who were mourning in verse 4. They were waiting for God to establish His righteous kingdom in Israel and remove the oppressive, pagan Romans. And Jesus came preaching that this kingdom had arrived in His own person.

Hunger for righteousness, then, is not simply a desire for personal sanctity. Nor should we limit it to a passion for social justice. In Jesus' context, it is both of these things, and more. It is a desire to see all things put "right," where "right" is defined by God's standards. It is a longing that all things—whether personal or social—should be rightly related to God and each other. It is a longing for the coming kingdom of God.

We are still left with a question: How will all this be accomplished? How does Jesus fulfill His promise to the hungry and thirsty, that they will be filled? As with a number of the Beatitudes, Jesus fulfills the Old Testament hopes, but in a way that people were not expecting.

The message of the rest of the New Testament is that Jesus established a kingdom in which "the righteous will live by faith" (Rom. 1:17). And He achieved this by dying. Through His sacrificial death,

Jesus finally satisfied those who hungered for righteousness. He paid the penalty for sin, so that all could be put right between God and man.

This was the last thing that Israel was expecting. They were hoping for a messiah who would restore the fortunes of the nation, drive out the pagan invaders, and establish his throne in Jerusalem. They did not realize that God's plan was about a worldwide kingdom, available to all—a kingdom that was spiritual rather than military.

This righteous kingdom, which Jesus established through His death and resurrection, will be finally and gloriously revealed when He comes again. Notice how the following passage from 2 Peter expresses this and uses ideas from Isaiah 51:1-6 (which we looked up earlier):

> But the day of the Lord will come like a thief. The heavens will disappear with a roar; the elements will be destroyed by fire, and the earth and everything in it will be laid bare.
>
> Since everything will be destroyed in this way, what kind of people ought you to be? You ought to live holy and godly lives as you look forward to the day of God and speed its coming. That day will bring about the destruction of the heavens by fire, and the elements will melt in the heat. But in keeping with his promise we are looking forward to a new heaven and a new earth, the home of righteousness.

—2 Peter 3:10-13 (emphasis added)

3. Good Living—Hunger and Satisfaction

One of the blessings of being part of God's kingdom is that our hunger for righteousness is satisfied. It is . . . and yet it isn't.

Through placing our trust in Jesus, we enter His righteous kingdom. Our sins are wiped away, and God regards us as righteous. However, we still await the time when our fallen, fundamentally unrighteous world is destroyed and a new, righteous order is created. We still live in what the New Testament calls "this present evil age."

In other words, even though our hunger for righteousness is satisfied in Christ, we still long for the time when the whole world will be put right—when every tongue will confess His lordship, and when all evil and injustice will be done away with. We still hunger and thirst for that day, and we cry, "Come, Lord Jesus, come!"

As with the other Beatitudes, this marks us out as different from the rest of the world. We aren't satisfied with the status quo, nor are we pessimistic about the future. We can long for righteousness in our world with a knowledge that one day it will surely be established through God's intervention.

We are blessed if we have this hunger, for we know it will be satisfied; indeed, we have already tasted something of that satisfaction in our own lives, with the righteousness we enjoy before God in Christ.

GOING FURTHER

1. List some things in the world and in our society that make you long for God's righteous kingdom.

2. What is "righteousness"?

3. How does Jesus satisfy "those who hunger and thirst for righteousness"?

4. Are there some things in your own life that you want put right? At home? At work?

5. We are very often complacent about evil and injustice and unrighteousness. Why do you think this is the case?

6. How should this Beatitude affect our attitude toward the evil/injustice in our own lives and in society?

The Return of the Merciful

"Blessed are the merciful,
for they will be shown mercy."
—Matthew 5:7

In a book called *The Religious Factor in Australian Life*, Gary Buhmer analyzes the results of an extensive "values survey" conducted in Australia in 1983. One part of the survey dealt with "tolerance" by asking people about their attitudes to various "undesirable" groups. People were asked: Would you object to your next-door neighbors being . . .

> people with criminal records; people of a different race; students; left-wing extremists; never-married mothers; heavy drinkers; people with large families; right-wing extremists; emotionally unstable people; members of minority religious sects or cults; immigrants/foreign workers; unemployed persons; aborigines; homosexuals.

The answers were analyzed according to the social and religious groupings of respondents, with an "index of tolerance" comparing the tolerance level of the groups. In the religious category, there were five groupings: 1) Roman Catholic, 2) Anglican, 3) "PMU" (Presbyterian, Methodist, Uniting), 4) "RWP" (Right-wing Protestants), 5) No religion.

 STARTING OUT

List the five groups in what you think would be their order of tolerance (list the most tolerant group first).

1.   2.   3.   4.   5.

The survey results were as follows (with the most tolerant first):

1. RWP (Right-wing Protestants)

2. Anglican

3. PMU (Presbyterian, Methodist, Uniting)

4. Roman Catholic

5. No religion

This result surprised everyone. The hardline, fundamentalist, "Bible-thumping" Christians turned out to be the most tolerant group by a significant margin. Those with no religion came last, also by a significant margin. We might well wonder why this is the case.

The Beatitude we turn to in this study is all about tolerance—or more precisely, mercy: "Blessed are the merciful, for they will be shown mercy." The theme of mercy keeps cropping up throughout Matthew's gospel. On two separate occasions, Jesus chides the Pharisees for not understanding the meaning of a verse about mercy from the Old Testament: "I desire mercy, not sacrifice" (see Matt. 9:9-13; 12:1-8). It seems that these words from Hosea 6 were important to Jesus. They lay at the heart of His mission—He had come to call sinners, not the righteous. To understand mercy the way Jesus understood mercy, we need to follow His advice—we need to go and learn what these words in Hosea mean!

1. The Hope—Mercy for Wayward Israel

Hosea was a prophet of doom. He came to Israel and Judah proclaiming a message of unremitting disaster because of their unfaithfulness to God. His message of judgment spilled over into his family life, with his wife and children serving as living illustrations of Israel's behavior and its consequences.

The adultery of Hosea's wife, Gomer, was a metaphor for Israel's unfaithfulness toward God. Hosea's children were given names such as "not loved" and "not my people" to demonstrate to everyone that God was not going to show mercy to Israel and Judah. God was going to disown them for all that they had done.

FINDING TRUTH

Read Hosea 6:4-10. (Note that "love" and "mercy" mean almost the same thing in the Old Testament. To love is to show compassion to someone in need, to be generous, regardless of whether the person deserves it or not. This, too, is the essence of mercy.)

1. What is Israel/Judah's "love" actually like?

2. What does God desire from Israel?

3. What does He see instead?

Now read Hosea 5:14–6:3.

4. Is there any future hope for Israel and Judah?

5. What will God's mercy to them be like?

6. How does this Old Testament hope shed light on what Jesus came to do (see Matt. 9:9-13)?

7. When Jesus came, what did He find in the leaders of Israel? Was it any different from Hosea's day (see Matt. 23:23-24)?

2. The Fulfillment—A Merciful Kingdom

As we have looked at Jesus' teaching on mercy and at its Old Testament background in Hosea, a picture has emerged of what Jesus meant when He proclaimed in the Beatitude, "Blessed are the merciful, for they will be shown mercy."

Israel looked forward to a time when God would return to them and revive them, showing them mercy after the punishments He had inflicted on them. Those punishments were a result of Israel's own *lack* of mercy, her disregard for justice and godliness, the superficiality of her love. She performed the right sacrifices and religious rituals but knew nothing of love and mercy.

When Jesus comes to bring the long-awaited mercy, He finds that little has changed. The Pharisees, who claimed to know the Scriptures, were not people of mercy. They were censorious and judgmental. They preferred to stand on their own "legalistic" righteousness rather than beg for God's undeserved mercy.

How different they were from the so-called "sinners" Jesus mixed with. These sinners knew that mercy was their only hope, and they were therefore people of mercy. They showed mercy to others because, unlike the Pharisees, they understood what mercy was and how much they needed it.

This is the meaning of Jesus' saying in Matthew 5. He is saying that only those who embrace *mercy as a lifestyle* will receive mercy. Only those who realize what mercy is and how much they need it, and who consequently are forgiving toward others, will seek and enter the Kingdom of Mercy that Jesus brings.

In fulfillment of the hope of Hosea, Jesus comes to "call sinners"; He comes as a doctor to the sick in Israel; He brings the long-awaited mercy. The rest of the New Testament rings with the news that this mercy is granted through His death on the Cross.

3. Good Living—The Mercy Principle

We are blessed indeed, according to Jesus, if we live our lives according to the mercy principle. If we pin our hopes on mercy, rather than on personal achievement, then entrance into His kingdom is ours for the taking. This is good living: being shown mercy by God and showing mercy to others.

However, Jesus' words also present a sobering challenge: If our lives are *not* characterized by mercy, have we understood our own need of mercy? The words of Jesus would suggest not.

 GOING FURTHER

1. How do most people think they can get right with God?

2. How does this Beatitude compare with this way of thinking?

3. In what ways could you be more merciful?

4. In what ways might this attitude be worked out in your church?

5. How should we deal with resentful feelings toward others?

Justice - the law getting what you deserve

Grace - not getting what you deserve.

Mercy - getting what you don't deser

giving someone a second chance, even when they don't deserve it.

pity + action = mercy

7

The Sight of the Pure

"Blessed are the pure in heart,
for they will see God."
—Matthew 5:8

Purity is about as exciting as a confirmation class. It conjures up images of little girls in white frocks wrapped in an aura of light and flowers. Purity is not an "in" word.

When we do stop to think about purity—not something modern Christians do very often—we usually think of sexual purity. We remember the dark, impure thoughts that have plagued us; we remember those times when perhaps our lack of purity made us think, "If Jesus had been here, I would have been ashamed to look Him in the face."

In linking purity of heart with seeing God, Jesus echoes our own deep feelings, as well as the experience of many people in the Bible. We know, almost instinctively, that our sin (or lack of purity) prevents us from approaching God openly and looking Him in the face. Or to put it another way, God's holiness keeps us away from Him. We can't approach Him.

This was how Isaiah felt when confronted with a revelation of God's glory in the temple. It was too much for him: "Woe to me! . . . I am ruined! For I am a man of unclean lips, and I live among a people of unclean lips, and my eyes have seen the King, the LORD Almighty" (Isa. 6:5). This was also the experience of Peter (Luke 5:1-11) and of Samson's parents (Judg. 13:22). When sinful humans are confronted by the presence of God, they become painfully aware of His blinding holiness and their own wretchedness.

As we shall see, Jesus' words in this Beatitude are by no means limited to sexual purity—in fact, they are not primarily about sexual purity. As we might expect, Jesus is drawing on a number of important Old Testament themes. Before we look more closely at these themes, we need to make a brief note about how this Beatitude is usually translated.

The Greek word translated "pure" (*katharos*) is the same word used to describe "clean" and "unclean" food. Jesus' words could just as well be translated: "Blessed are the *clean* in heart, for they will see God." This is how His hearers would have heard it—they would have associated Jesus' words with the religious practices of first-century Judaism.

In order to understand this Beatitude, then, we need to know a little about this distinction between clean and unclean.

1. The Hope—A Purified Israel

Under the Law of Moses, various areas of life were affected by clean/unclean regulations—eating certain foods (Lev. 11:43-47), touching dead or unclean animals or people (Num. 19:11-22), contracting various diseases (Lev. 13:1-3), and having a discharge of fluid from the body (Lev. 12:1-4). These were just some of the circumstances that rendered an Israelite "unclean."

Those who contracted some form of ritual or ceremonial defilement were not able to worship at the temple. God was holy, and His dwelling place was holy. There could be no contact between anyone or anything that was "unclean" and the Holy One of Israel. Unclean persons were excluded from drawing near to God until they were purified or cleansed (usually by some form of ritual washing or sacrifice).

However, the distinction between clean and unclean did not apply only to ceremonial and ritual matters. Let us look at the passage in Psalm 24 that Jesus appears to have drawn on for this Beatitude.

 FINDING TRUTH

Read Psalm 24:1-6.

1. Who may approach God at His "holy place" (the temple)?

2. Do you see any parallels between this psalm and Jesus' words in Matthew 5:8?

Read Ezekiel 36:22-32.

3. How had Israel treated God?

4. How does God intend to deal with Israel's sinfulness or "uncleanness"?

2. The Fulfillment—Clean Hearts, Clear Sight

In Jesus' time (which was 1,000 years after David's Psalm 24), the Pharisees focused very much on obedience to the legal, ceremonial precepts regarding cleanness and uncleanness. In fact, over the centuries an abundance of additional prohibitions and regulations had accumulated, and these "traditions of the elders," as they were called, were followed with equal rigor.

The Pharisees' zeal for obedience to an *external* code of often trivial regulations brought them into conflict with Jesus.

 FINDING TRUTH

Read Matthew 15:1-20.

1. What is Jesus' attitude toward being "clean" or "unclean"?

2. How is this different from the attitude of the Pharisees?

Now read Matthew 23:25-28.

3. What is the error of the Pharisees and teachers of the Law?

Many of us have grown up with an interpretation of this Beatitude that goes something like this: If you can manage to remove impure thoughts and feelings from your mind, then you will be able to see God's face in prayer—on the back of your eyelids, as it were. Our impurity prevents us from seeing this vision of God, but if we confess all our sins and avoid impure thoughts and behavior, then we will enjoy unspoiled communion with God.

These ideas may or may not be true in themselves, but they are almost certainly not what Jesus meant when He spoke to His disciples on the mountainside.

As we have seen, the prevailing religious sentiment of the day was that if you were ceremonially clean (externally), you could worship God at the temple. The Pharisees might have said: "Blessed are the outwardly clean, for they shall approach God at the temple."

Jesus says something very different. He reminds His audience of what God really wants in the way of cleanness: Blessed are the clean *in heart,* for they will *see God.*

As we saw from Psalm 24, God was always interested in people who were pure not just externally, but internally—people who were *pure in heart.* We shouldn't think that somehow the Old Testament God was satisfied with external observance of rules, while the New Testament God wanted a religion of the heart. The importance of a right *attitude* to God is taught throughout the Old Testament.

Jesus reminds His hearers of this. In contrast to the dominant emphasis of the time (which was on external observance), Jesus reaffirms the importance of heart commitment. This theme runs throughout the Sermon on the Mount. In the rest of chapter 5, Jesus teaches His disciples how their righteousness must exceed the legalism of the Pharisees and the teachers of the Law. It is not enough to simply refrain from the physical act of murder; the people of the kingdom must have the right attitude as well—in this case, not being angry (5:21-22). The same is true of adultery, divorce, oaths, and revenge. In chapter 6, Jesus contrasts the hypocrisy of those who do their "acts of righteousness" in public with those who do them in secret and whose reward is from God.

For Jesus, then, the important thing is not being clean externally, but being clean *in heart*.

But there is more. As we saw in Ezekiel 36, the Old Testament prophets looked forward to a time when God would give His people a new, clean heart that was inclined to obey Him. Jeremiah prophesied the same thing when he envisaged a New Covenant in which God would put His "law in their minds and write it on their hearts" (Jer. 31:33).

Jesus brings in this New Covenant between God and His people. Through Christ's blood, our hearts can now be cleansed. Our sins can be wiped away, and we can approach God with confidence.

In this new kingdom, inner cleanness does not simply give us access to the temple worship—it gives us access to the very face of God. Under the Old Covenant, no one could come into God's presence in the Holy of Holies except the high priest, and he was only allowed in once a year under strict conditions. Under the New Covenant, the curtain separating us from the Holy of Holies is torn asunder. Because of what Jesus has done, the barrier to full fellowship with God has been removed, and every believer may now approach Him with confidence. The writer to the Hebrews summarizes it all beautifully:

> *Therefore, brothers, since we have confidence to enter the Most Holy Place by the blood of Jesus, by a new and living way opened for us through the curtain, that is, his body, and since we have a great priest over the house of God, let us draw near to God with a sincere heart in full assurance of faith, having our hearts sprinkled to cleanse us from a guilty conscience and having our bodies washed with pure water.*
> —Hebrews 10:19-22

This is the message of the Gospel: that because of Jesus' death, our sinful, unclean hearts no longer prevent us from having fellowship with God. Our hearts can be cleansed.

3. Good Living—Beneath the Veneer

As people of this New Covenant (i.e., those whose hearts have been cleansed), we can now see God, even if it is only in part. As Paul says: "Now we see but a poor reflection as in a mirror; then we shall see face to face. Now I know in part; then I shall know fully, even as I am fully known" (1 Cor. 13:12). John expresses the same thought: "Dear friends, now we are children of God, and what we will be has not yet been made known. But we know that when he appears, we shall be like him, for we shall see him as he is. Everyone who has this hope in him purifies himself, just as he is pure" (1 John 3:2-3).

Jesus' kingdom requires a change of heart, a change that He Himself achieves. It's a kingdom in which the heart matters more than the appearance. Once again, this contrasts radically with the world around us. Modern society is obsessed with appearances, with maintaining a veneer of respectability over the corruption that lurks beneath.

The good life is to be found by abandoning this pretense, by getting a clean heart (available in Jesus), and by dealing with God and each other on a "heart basis."

 GOING FURTHER

1. What do you think Jesus means when He says: "For I tell you that unless your righteousness surpasses that of the Pharisees and teachers of the law, you will certainly not enter the kingdom of heaven" (Matt. 5:20)?

2. In what sense do we "see God" as Christians?

3. In what ways are we tempted to emphasize the external over the internal?

   ▲ at home

   ▲ at church

   ▲ at work/study

4. Are there any areas in your life in which you are like the Pharisees—doing the right thing outwardly but with the wrong attitude/motivation?

5. What impure attitudes or behavior do you need to clean up?

6. Choose one area you would like to work on; pray about it.

8

The Family of the Peacemakers

> *"Blessed are the peacemakers,*
> *for they will be called sons of God."*
> —Matthew 5:9

In the days of Jeremiah, the leaders of Israel proclaimed "Peace, peace" when there was no peace (Jer. 6:14; 8:11). This can be our reaction to the hopeful sentiments of world leaders, media commentators, and miscellaneous idealists who promise that lasting peace in our time is possible—and indeed not far off.

The remarkable events in Eastern Europe in the late 1980s, the reform of apartheid in South Africa, the improvement in relations between Moscow and Washington, the prospect of significant disarmament—these have all been seen as signs of a new age of peace, when people will stop fighting each other and work together in harmony.

These positive signs are certainly to be welcomed, but do they herald a new era? World history would suggest not. No sooner do we solve one arena of conflict than another breaks out. Even during periods we might designate as peaceful, conflict continues; there were fifty major international conflicts between 1945 and 1965.

What does Jesus mean in pronouncing a blessing on the "peacemakers"? Is He establishing a kind of first-century Nobel Peace Prize? Or is He talking about mending the fences with your quarrelsome neighbor?

1. The Hope—Peace in Their Time

The modern meaning of the word *peace* is significantly different from its meaning in Old Testament times. A recent edition of the *Concise*

Oxford Dictionary lists among its meanings for peace: "freedom from or cessation of war; freedom from civil disorder; quiet, tranquillity; mental calm; a state of friendliness or quietness." Modern peace, in other words, is characterized by a lack of conflict (whether military, civil, or mental).

In the Old Testament, however, peace had a much broader and more positive meaning. Peace was not simply the absence of conflict, but the positive experience of well-being, safety, and prosperity. Peace was the opposite not so much of war as of any conflict or situation that affected the well-being of the Israelite community.

Once again, the kingships of David and Solomon were the high point of Old Testament peace. In this period, Israel experienced prosperity and safety from their enemies. They were in the land God had chosen for them, enjoying its bounty, at one with each other and with their God. This was real peace.

However, the pattern we have seen emerge in a number of our studies also applies to Israel's experience of peace. The high point was David and Solomon, but from the latter part of Solomon's reign onward, the deterioration was steady and tragic. Because of her consistent apostasy, Israel's peace was shattered. The kingdom itself split in two, and the ten northern tribes ("Israel") and the two southern tribes ("Judah") bickered and fought until the northern tribes were wiped out by Assyria. The communal "good life" that was the essence of Israel's peace was eroded and finally destroyed by God as a consequence of Israel's rebellion against Him.

As we have also seen in previous studies, the sin and judgment of Israel was accompanied by a prophetic hope for a better future. The prophets looked forward to a time when the poor would be liberated, when there would be comfort and restoration for Israel, when the mourners would again rejoice, when the meek would come into their inheritance, when God's righteous kingdom would be established, and when mercy would be shown to wayward Israel and she would be cleansed from all her sin.

The same thought is expressed with regard to peace.

FINDING TRUTH

Read Psalm 85.

1. What are the characteristics of the "peace" that God promises His people?

Read Isaiah 52:7-10.

2. What will the peace be like when it comes?

Read Ezekiel 37:24-28.

3. What will God do for wayward Israel?

2. The Fulfillment—The Prince of Peace

Jesus came announcing that the long-awaited kingdom of God (i.e., the kingdom of peace) had arrived. He came to do what Isaiah and Ezekiel had prophesied: to cleanse God's people, to bring salvation, to establish a New Covenant of peace in which God's people experienced His blessing.

In this New Covenant, as in the Old, God is the great peacemaker—not in the sense of calling a truce but by defeating Satan and establishing a kingdom of safety and well-being for those who share in the victory with Him. This message is repeated throughout the New Testament:

> *He forgave us all our sins, having cancelled the written code, with its regulations, that was against us and that stood opposed to us; he took it away, nailing it to the cross. And having disarmed the powers and authorities, he made a public spectacle of them, triumphing over them by the cross.*
>
> —Colossians 2:13b-15

> *For God was pleased to have all his fullness dwell in him, and through him to reconcile to himself all things . . . by* making peace through his blood, *shed on the cross.*
>
> —Colossians 1:19-20 (emphasis added)

> *Therefore, since we have been justified through faith,* we have peace with God *through our Lord Jesus Christ. . . . If,* when we were God's enemies, *we were reconciled to him through the death of his Son, how much more, having been reconciled, shall we be saved through his life!*
>
> —Romans 5:1, 10 (emphasis added)

God makes peace with us—His enemies—by paying for our sin. He comes to those in rebellion against Him and reconciles them to Himself. He restores our relationships with each other as well. Ephesians 2 teaches us that the dividing wall of hostility between Jew and Gentile has been broken down in Christ. Through Christ's reconciling death on the Cross, there has been an "outbreak" of peace:

> *For he himself is our peace, who has made the two one and has destroyed the barrier, the dividing wall of hostility, by abolishing in his flesh the law with its commandments and regulations. His purpose was to create in himself one new man out of the two, thus making peace.*
>
> —Ephesians 2:14-15

In this Beatitude, Jesus says that those who pursue peace will be blessed, for they will be called "sons of God." Those who want to be part of the kingdom of the Prince of Peace must themselves be people of peace. They must commit themselves to "making peace" as a general rule of life. Then they will be "sons of God" in two senses:

▲ They will become *part of God's family.* Like Old Testament Israel, which God designated "my son," the members of the kingdom will become God's sons and daughters, born "not of natural descent, nor of human decision or a husband's will, but born of God" (John 1:13).

▲ They will be acting in the family likeness of God; like Him, they will be peacemakers. This is one of the ways the phrase "sons of" is used in the Bible (e.g., Luke 6:35). Any son is like his father, and we will be like our Father in heaven if we pursue peace.

3. Good Living—People of Peace

What does it mean for us to be peacemakers? If what we have said so far is true, then it must mean more than simply "not fighting." Making peace means restoring harmony and well-being to broken relationships and situations.

If we are to be like God the great Peacemaker, then our peacemaking must include evangelism—that is, making peace between God and those around us. We should call on people to stop their rebellion against God and be reconciled to Him.

As members of the kingdom of peace, we are uniquely equipped for peacemaking. We hunger for righteousness, but we also understand the need for mercy and grace (see studies 1, 5, and 6).

Being peacemakers is a matter of attitude and orientation. It involves being willing to reconcile, to make the first move toward an adversary, and not to stand on our own rights. In other words, it is being like God, who made the first move toward us, His enemies, to reconcile us to Himself.

"As far as it depends on you," says Paul, "live at peace with everyone" (Rom. 12:18; see James 3:17-18). This is the radically good life that Jesus teaches: to sow peace in a world full of turmoil, ambition, and strife.

 **GOING FURTHER**

1.   What is "peace" in the Bible?

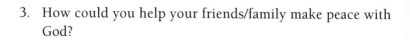

2. Some of Jesus' audience could have been "nationalists" who favored a military rebellion against the Romans. How do you think they would have reacted to this Beatitude?

3. How could you help your friends/family make peace with God?

4. Can you think of ways in which you could be a peacemaker

   ▲ at home?

   ▲ at church?

   ▲ with your friends?

   ▲ at work/school?

3. What particular situations provoke an aggressive response in you? How could you work against this?

The Joy of the Persecuted

"Blessed are those who are persecuted
  because of righteousness,
  for theirs is the kingdom of heaven.

"Blessed are you when people insult you, persecute you and falsely
say all kinds of evil against you because of me. Rejoice and be glad,
because great is your reward in heaven, for in the same way they per-
secuted the prophets who were before you."
                                                    —Matthew 5:10-12

Our love of popularity is insatiable. Few forces mold us more pow-
erfully. We long to be affirmed, encouraged, approved of, respected,
praised. And when we are not, our defenses rise in various forms—
we go on the attack, we run away, we make excuses, we flagellate ourselves, we bluster, we clown around.

Our love of popularity is nowhere better illustrated than in our
slavish attendance to "fashion." As Thoreau so whimsically put it,
"The head monkey at Paris puts on a traveler's cap, and all the mon-
keys in America do the same." Even at the basic level of simply
clothing our bodies, our choices are largely dictated by our desire to
be accepted by others.

The desire for popularity affects nearly every aspect of our lives—
the way we speak, the movies we see, the opinions we express (or
refrain from expressing), our behavior when with others, and so on.

Popularity is a tyrant. It enslaves us to doing things that we don't
really want to do. And because of the fickleness of the mob, it's very
hard to keep up. By the time you have finally bought your Hawaiian
shirt, it is no longer "in."

This last Beatitude is double-barreled. It starts with the usual formula: "Blessed are those who . . . (live this way), for . . . (this will happen to them)." However, Jesus reinforces the point by repeating a personal version of the blessing: "Blessed are *you* when people insult you. . . ."

In many ways, this Beatitude is the simplest of all. Its ideas are stark and challenging, but not difficult to follow.

[handwritten: My Question: ... the ... persecution, ... some exam...]

1. The Old Testament Example

"Rejoice and be glad," says Jesus, "for in the same way they persecuted the prophets who were before you." In the Old Testament, there was an oft-repeated pattern—the people would sin; God would send one of His prophets; and the people would reject the words of the prophet and persecute him.

[handwritten left margin: My Question:] *[handwritten: Why does persecution or what is it the motivates people to persecute others]*

▲ **FINDING TRUTH** *[handwritten: Because it contradicts sinful nature]*

Read Jeremiah 20:1-12.

1. What is Jeremiah's initial reaction to the persecution?

   *[handwritten: anger, retaliates & curses Pashur, then a complaint with God.
   Note: this is the first recorded acts of violence to ward Jeremiah. Jeremiah's complaint to God is the last]*

2. What is his hope for the future? (vv. 11-12)

   [handwritten: His persecutors will fall, the will Lord righteously judge - ...in the end he see his redeamer (Jo 19:2]

2. Continued in the New Testament . . .

The people of Jeremiah's day treated him poorly. They threatened to kill him and on another occasion lowered him into a muddy cistern to starve to death.

Interestingly enough, when we skip forward to the New Testament, we find that the people of Jesus' day treated the Old Testament prophets such as Jeremiah with reverence and respect. Their words were read in the synagogue and learned by heart.

But when Jesus came preaching the same message of repentance, and indeed fulfilling all that the prophets had looked forward to, He was hated, reviled, spat upon, and finally killed.

 FINDING TRUTH

Read Matthew 5:10-12.

- to face or confront
n-VIZ-ig
- to form any image in ones mind

1. As Jesus elaborates in verses 11-12, what does He envisage will be involved in persecution?

A blessing, A reward a benediction. Those persecuted reciving the Kingdom of heaven

What do you see pictured?

or 'The righteous!'

Read the parallel passage in Luke 6:22-23.

2. Does it add anything?

hatred, exclusion, is more harsh you can have friends persecute you, (pass judgement), but still have a relationship with you. ~~The~~ A greater form of persecution would come from exclusion.

Read Matt: 10:22

3. <u>Persecution</u>, by itself, is no virtue. We may be persecuted because we are objectionable, argumentative people who always ask for a fight. Jesus is talking about being persecuted <u>"because of righteousness."</u> Review your notes from our study of Matthew 5:6 (study 5). What did we conclude that "righteousness" meant in this context?

general: righteousness – getting right with God
context: the desire to be free from sin (
to pursue justification & sanctification

4. In Matthew 5, compare verse 10 with verse 11. What slight variation is there in the reason for persecution? What does this comparison tell us about the "righteousness"?

10. because of righteousness
11. because of me. more personal
Christ & righteousness are one in the sam

5. Jesus says that we are to rejoice when this persecution for righteousness comes. For what two reasons are we to rejoice?

in time we will be rewarded with
something greater (1) great is your reward in
(2) YOUR PERSECUTION IS
LIKE THE PROPHETS B

3. Good Living—Truly Alive

This last Beatitude is a fitting way to conclude. Having outlined a set of radical "kingdom values," it is no surprise that Jesus finishes by warning His disciples that they will be persecuted <u>for living this way.</u> People will hate us for living in a way that proclaims truth and exposes falsehood. By setting out to be *different* in the ways that Jesus teaches, we face the inevitability of conflict.

not just for being righteous, but for all the beattitudes

We will continue to experience the strange perversity of persecution. Every generation wants to revere and claim as their own the great prophets of the past, and yet at the same time reviles the prophets of the present. In the New Testament, the Pharisees revered Moses and all the ancient prophets yet rejected John the Baptist, and then Jesus. Today, evangelical Christians love to sing the hymns of the Wesley brothers and read the works of John Bunyan and J. C.

Ryle. Yet in their own day, these men were hated and persecuted, even by Christians. We must expect this. If we preach the truth and call on people to repent, we will be persecuted.

Note, once again, how Jesus turns conventional expectation upside down. This sort of persecution, He says, is really worth having! Being persecuted for righteousness is great; rejoice and be glad about it, because God, who sees all, has reserved for you the kingdom of heaven.

It seems a strange way to put it, but the persecuted person is truly free. Having reached the stage of being so unpopular as to be persecuted, he is free from the tyranny of group popularity. He is free to do what he's always wanted to do but has been afraid to because of the crowd. The persecuted person doesn't need to worry about what others will think of him, since they already think the worst.

Moreover, the persecuted person is truly alive. There is an old saying: "Even a dead dog can swim with the tide." To swim against the tide, you have to be alive and kicking. Following the leader requires neither thought nor effort. You can hang the latest fashions on a mannequin or a socialite—they have equal qualifications and equal quantities of life. Taking a stand and being different requires you to *live*.

ARE WE ~~THE~~ PROPHETS OF THIS AGE?

from: *If we aren't suffering, ~~this~~ persecution at all, does that mean...? ——→ ②*

GOING FURTHER

Write down some recent examples of when you were faced with taking a stand for righteousness. What did you do in each case? What happened as a result . . .

▲ where you live?

ASK FOR EVERYONE TO RECAP. THIS *entire* STUDY

SEE MY NOTES ——→

~~▲ with your neighbors?~~

1. Is this beattitude any different than the others?

2. Notice how this beattitude has the same promise as the first one " poor in spirit" Kingdom of heaven why

▲ where you work/study?

▲ with your family?

▲ socializing (at a party/with friends)?

▲ in your financial affairs?

2. If we are suffering no persecution *at all*, is it reasonable to con-clude that we have not aligned ourselves with "righteous-ness"? (Compare Luke 6:26 and 2 Tim. 3:12.)

3. When we are being persecuted, what does it mean, in practi-cal terms, to rejoice?

FAITHWALK
BIBLE STUDIES

Ask your local bookstore about these other
FaithWalk Bible Studies

Beginnings
Eden and Beyond: Genesis 1–11

Daniel
Our Faithful God

Isaiah
The Road to God

Deuteronomy
The Lord Your God

Galatians
The Gospel of Grace

Ephesians
Our Blessings in Christ

1 Timothy
The Household of God

Notes

First 3   Poor
          Morn   } Humble, needs
          Meek

Thirst for Righteousness
merciful
pure in heart
peace makers
persecuted

To some, at first thought, the beatitud
call to is so high that ~~folks~~ folks have
dismissed it as being unrealistic. But
we can trust that though these are
~~to~~ tough standards, in a world of s
that these demands cannot be m
in our own power,

Notes

Notes

Notes

About Matthias Media

This Bible study guide, part of the *FaithWalk Bible Studies,* was originally developed and published in Australia by Matthias Media. Matthias Media is an evangelical publisher focusing on producing resources for Christian ministry. For further information about Matthias Media products, visit their website at: www.matthiasmedia.com.au; or contact them by E-mail at: matmedia@ozemail.com.au; or by fax at: 61-2-9662-4289.